A Family guide to gun safety

by
Christopher Ford

Published by White Feather Press. (www.whitefeatherpress.com)

ISBN 978-1618081339

Printed in the United States of America

White Feather Press

Reafferming Faith in God, Family and Country

FOREWORD

Even before our country was officially founded, firearms had been a part of American culture. Our country was based on the fact that our rights and freedoms come from God. In our Bill of Rights, the founding fathers made the right to keep and bear arms second only to the freedom of speech. Thomas Jefferson, John Adams, George Mason, Samuel Adams and so many others, labored tirelessly to create a new nation with laws free from the tyranny of the old world. A place where the government would represent the people, not repress them.

Firearms are, first and foremost, a tool to secure your life and the lives of others, against any aggressor. They are also used for hunting and sport, but if used irresponsibly can have grave and unwanted consequences. Children are our greatest gift, and being a parent is our biggest responsibility. As firearms owners we have a duty to keep our firearms always secured and locked away from children. As parents we have an obligation to teach our children safety measures when it comes to firearms in our homes or if they encounter them elsewhere. Please spend time with your children going over the lessons in this book, because safety can only be truly enhanced thru education.

Paul J Buffoni, President, Bravo Company MFG, Inc.

Your father and mother want you to know that we love you very much. The Lord has entrusted us with your well-being, and that is the greatest gift we have ever received.

Part of looking out for your well-being is making sure that you are safe both inside our home and outside our home.

...or when we are hunting and fishing.

But you must know that one of the most important rules in a home with guns is that you are never allowed to touch a gun without asking Mommy and Daddy first, every time.

Even outside of our home, if you ever see a gun, you have to ask mommy and daddy if it's OK for you to touch it.

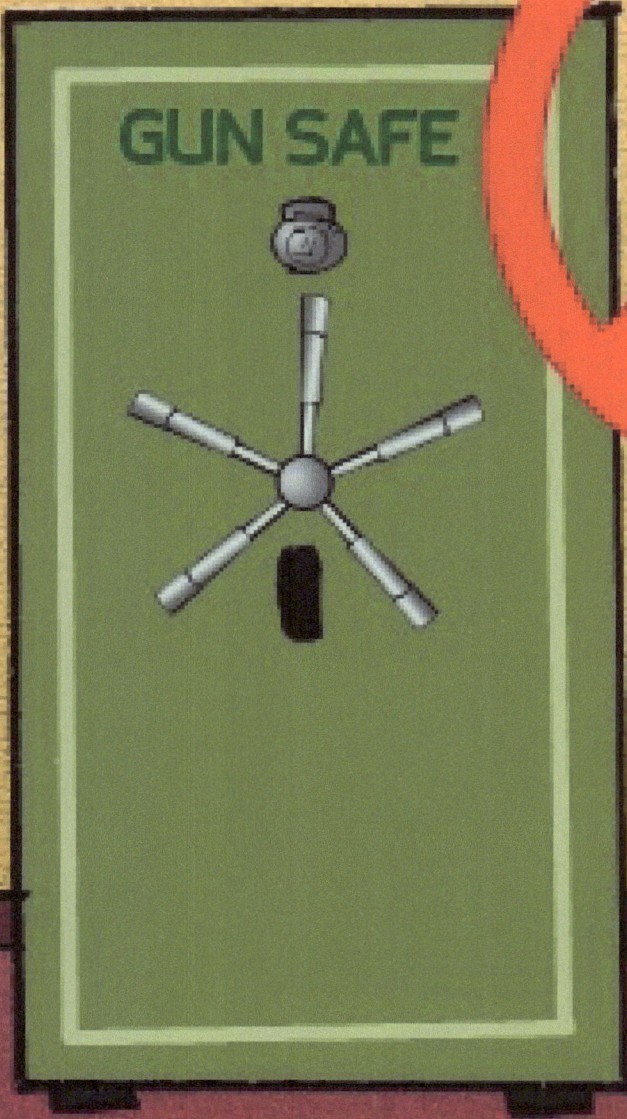

You are NEVER allowed to touch a gun without our permission.

Sometimes, Mommy and Daddy will say no if you ask to touch a gun. If we say no, we will find something else fun for you to do.

GUN SAFE
So always remember, when you see a gun, no matter where you are,
DO NOT touch it unless Mommy or Daddy say it's okay.
Follow this rule, and we can live safely and happily.

What have we learned?

Answer the questions below correctly and have your parents fill out the completion certificate on the next page. Then you can hang it on your wall or your refrigerator to show your friends and family that you are safe around guns!

Answer True or False (circle one)

1. There are many families in America who safely own guns.
   - -True
   - - False

2. Firearms are, first and foremost, a tool to secure your life and the lives of others, against any aggressor.
   - -True
   - -False

3. Your mother and father love you very much.
   - -True
   - - False

4. Guns can be fun when used safely.
   - - True
   - - False

5. You should never touch a gun unless your parents say it's okay.
   - - True
   - - False

6. When you see a gun, and no one else is there, you may touch the gun,
   - - True
   - - False

Parents: The answer key is on the last page of this book.

Certificate of Safety

This certificate is awarded to

_____

and shows they know how to never touch guns unless mother
and father say it's okay.

Certified Safe!

ABOUT THE AUTHOR

Chris Ford grew up on a farm in the Ozark Mountains of Missouri. He spent lots of time hunting and fishing with his father and grandfather all over the Midwest.

Chris holds a degree in aerospace engineering from the university of Missouri Science and Technology. He lives in North Carolina with his beautiful wife Jennifer, their daughter Ainsley and son Austin. He plays electric guitar at his local church every Sunday, enjoys racecars, hot rods, working with firearms as well as hunting and fishing.

Chris created this book to help his children and children everywhere understand the importance of gun safety.

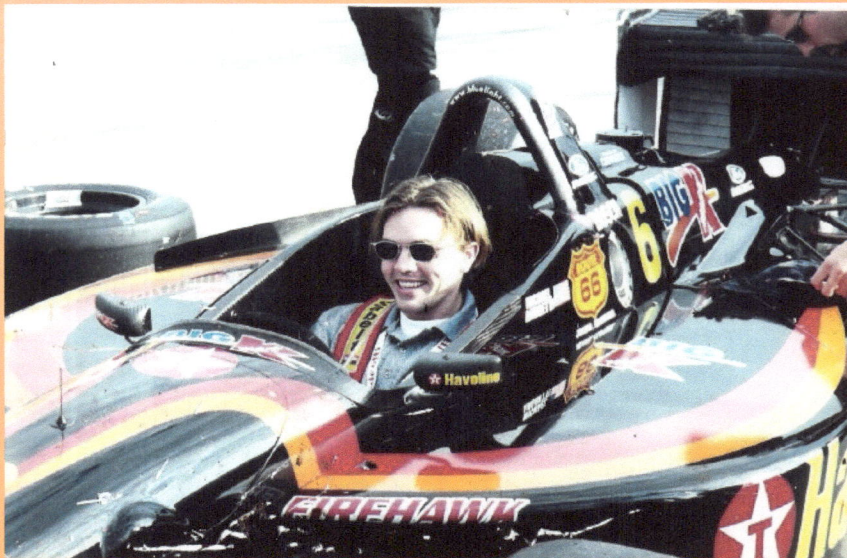

The author at Michigan International Speedway in 2003.

Test key:
1 – True
2 – True
3 – True
4 – True
5 – True
6 – False